Individualize to Maximize Children's Behaviors

Easy-to-Use, Reusable, and Customizable Templates that Help Children Cope and Self-monitor in an Interactive Way."

SHERYL FOYE, PSY.D.

Copyright © 2014, 2015 Sheryl Foye, Psy.D.

All rights reserved.

ISBN: 1523331011
ISBN-13: 978-1523331017

Introduction

I developed this book in hopes of providing educators, other school professionals, and even caregivers, with practical, customizable, and easy-to-implement tools for assisting children in managing their own behavior. These tools are designed to promote independent use of coping strategies and to encourage self-monitoring of emotions and behaviors. The design of each tool is clearly-presented, well-organized, and easy-to-understand at a glance. All components are available for the reader to create templates for a number of tools that can be customized for use again and again to meet a variety of emotional and behavioral needs. Furthermore, additional components are included for easily tracking essential data to ensure that progress is being made.

These tools allow educators to keep track of data easily using simple Velcro pieces that transfer from the chart's back to the front when strategies are used or target behaviors are observed. Additionally, these tools can promote the generalization of skills to natural settings (i.e., from therapeutic settings to the classroom). There is an expectation that Individualized Education Plan (IEP) goals and objectives include criteria for not only developing a specific skill, but also for demonstrating that skill within natural environments. These tools help promote the carryover of students' learned skills to real-life settings unobtrusively. By incorporating visuals and tangible chips, verbalizations can be minimized and nonverbal signals can be used instead, allowing fewer power struggles and less attention to be drawn to the child. Finally, these tools are accessible to and easily implemented by busy school staff. More specifically, feedback to the student is immediate and the data tracking is quick to "record." With all of the demands and expectations that educators and service providers have on them, they need simple, quick ways for reinforcing skills, recording data, and tailoring methods to meet individual student needs.

This book is divided into four different sections: 1) Coping Skill Tools, 2) Behavior Charts/Self-Monitoring Tools, 3) Data Recording Sheets/Home School Communication Notes, and 4) Rewards. The format of the book is as follows: a strategy is named, a description of how it should be implemented follows, then materials are provided to create the strategy or tool template with accompanying pieces and/or chips. An "example" is also provided for each of the coping skill tools and the behavior charts/self-monitoring plans in order to show what the template could look like once it is fully customized. Finally, sheets are provided to record data obtained from using the behavior charts/self-monitoring tools, which can be communicated with home, and reward information provides reward ideas and ensures a tracking mechanism for reward receipt.

Templates in the coping skill and behavior charts/self-monitoring tools sections are designed to be laminated (gluing them first on cardstock provides even more durability) so that they are reuseable. Despite being designed to be reusable, they also are designed to be easy to tailor to each child's needs by providing an assortment of chips as well as numerous visuals for strategies and target behaviors. By making the target behaviors interchangeable on all of the charts, each one is easy to adapt in order to make changes in target behaviors or behavioral goals for daily and/or weekly requirements. Furthermore, adhering target behaviors, strategies, and chips to each of the tools using Velcro allows adults to re-use the templates by simply changing the target behavior(s) or strategies and by removing chips. (When applying Velcro, maximize your ability to re-use the materials by placing the hook Velcro on the templates and the loop Velcro on the pieces that attach (i.e., target behaviors, chips, and strategies)). These velcroed chips also allow data to be tracked easily in-the-moment. A chip is simply added or removed without further effort. Once criteria is met, the data can then be transferred to the data tracking sheets, which also serve as home-school communication notes in order to keep caregivers informed of progress at school. These simple data tracking sheets also can be used as a supplement to gather and record data over time.

Finally, a section is provided for reward ideas and data-tracking slips are provided to track what rewards are given and when they are delivered. Rewards can be pivotal in determining a plan's effectiveness. If the reward is undesirable to a student or has lost its appeal, then the student is likely to become less interested in working toward it. Moreover, if a reward is not provided consistently or ever, it can impede a plan's effectiveness entirely. Some home-school notes also allow for data to be recorded regarding rewards in order to make plans more flexible for the adult using them. Because of this flexibility, one can also tie the plan into existing classroom positive reinforcement plans by using existing classroom reinforcers. The tools in this book are designed for your use to promote positive behavior. However, please note that these tools cannot stand alone. The most important piece of their effectiveness is your consistent implementation and follow through.

Guidelines for Using These Tools

1. **Discuss the selected coping skill tool or self-monitoring plan with the student.** By having this discussion, the student will know what to expect and will understand his role in using the plan or tool. Furthermore, with the coping skill tools, allow the student to practice using it prior to implementation.

2. **It is ok to give one simple reminder, especially in the first few weeks of a plan, about what the target behavior is before, for example, removing a chip (i.e., on the Think Chart).** If the first reminder does not work immediately, do not engage in power struggles about goals or losing chips. Simply remind him of the goal he is not demonstrating (i.e., "Sam, you need to use a 2nd grade voice.") and say, "That costs a chip." Ignore any further attempts in the moment. Wait for a calm moment much later or the next day, if you feel discussion is necessary.

3. **Give genuine, specific praise when target behaviors are exhibited.** Be sure to acknowledge when students are showing positive behaviors regardless of the plan that you are using. This praise should be clear and descriptive, describing what you see/hear or feel.

4. **Decide with the student when he will receive his reward and establish a consistent schedule.** In particular, discuss which day of the week and what time that day (i.e., during before schoolwork, at snack time, at the end of the day, just before dismissal, etc.) he will receive his reward. Depending on the plan, providing the reward at the end of the week usually makes the most sense; however, it should be noted that younger students and students with greater challenges may be more motivated by receiving rewards more immediately at first. For example, the requirements for reward eligibility might be daily

in the beginning stages of plan implementation. Once buy-in has been achieved, then reward eligibility requirements could increase to being eligible for a reward every other day. After another few weeks of continuous success on the plan, reward eligibility requirements could increase to being eligible for a reward on a weekly basis. Since delaying gratification can be more challenging for some students, a graduated plan for increasing reward eligibility requirements could be useful. Regardless of the final decision, it is important for the student to be able to anticipate and expect when rewards will be allotted.

5. **Whenever possible, avoid using tangible rewards.** Tangible rewards might include toys, knick knacks, etc. In cases where one must use them, once success has been achieved and intrinsic motivation has developed, different rewards should be considered.

6. **Ensure success in the initial stages of implementing the plan.** Be sure that the student meets reward eligibility requirements to attain his reward for the 1st 3 days (if daily reward) or weeks (if weekly reward) of the plan so that he becomes invested. This may mean that you have to be more lenient than you would like to be at first; however, the program can only be successful if he feels good about it and is excited about it. So as difficult as this is, please trust me! It will pay off in the end!! A word of caution: this means that you will need to be careful about removing chips (i.e., Think Chart) too quickly or too easily so that you don't run out of chips right away and then have nothing to use for the rest of the day.

7. **Never expect perfection; always leave room for bad days.** Everyone has a bad day, so build in that understanding with the plan. In other words, don't expect students to be able to show target behaviors 100% of the time. Instead, expect it 4 out of 5 days of the week for weekly plans, for example. Or for daily plans, expect 15 out of 24 checkmarks, or at least 1 chip still left or 2 out of 3 stars, etc. See individual plans for more specifics.

8. **When changing the criteria for meeting a goal, gradually make it more difficult for him to meet the requirements**. For example, you might say, "Now you need to earn 10 stars instead of 8 in order to meet your weekly requirement." (for the Stars chart). Only increase the demands in small increments and ensure that he has reached the set goal for several days/weeks in a row before changing the plan again.

References

The following is a list of resources that I found useful when creating these intervention ideas. They provide the empirical support for substantiating the approach taken in these intervention tools. These references also will provide the reader with further resources to review.

Barnett, D., & Bell, S. (1999). *Designing preschool interventions: A practitioner's guide.* New York: Guilford Press.

Bronson, M. (2000). *Self-regulation in early childhood: Nature and nurture*. New York: Guilford Press.

Dawson, P., & Guare, R. (2004). *Executive skills in children and adolescents: A practical guide to assessment and intervention*. New York: Guilford Press.

Dawson, P., & Guare, R. (2009). *Smart but Scattered*. New York: Guilford Press.

Essential components of RTI: A closer look at Response to Intervention. (2010). Washington, D.C.: National Center on Response to Intervention.

Madrigal, S., & Winner, M. (2008). *Superflex: A superhero social thinking curriculum*. San Jose, CA: Think Social Publishing.

Madrigal, S. (2008). *Superflex takes on Rock Brain and the team of Unthinkables: A new beginning*. San Jose, CA: Think Social Publishing, Inc.

O'leary, K., Becker, W., Evans, M., & Saudargas, R. (1969). A token reinforcement program in a public school: A replication and systematic analysis1. *Journal of Applied Behavior Analysis*, 3-13.

Rao, S. M., & Gagie, B. (2006). Learning through seeing and doing: Visual supports for children with autism. *TEACHING Exceptional Children*, *38*(6), 26-33.

Thomas, A. (1995). Ensuring Quality Interventions. In *Best practices in school psychology, III* (3rd ed., pp. 485-500). Washington, DC: National Association of School Psychologists.

Thomas, A. (1995). Planning Interventions for Students with Attention Disorders. In *Best practices in school psychology, III* (3rd ed., pp. 987-998). Washington, DC: National Association of School Psychologists.

What Is A Responsive Classroom Time-Out? (November, 2014). Retrieved from https://www.responsiveclassroom.org/article/positive-time-out

Wielkiewicz, R. (1995). *Behavior management in the schools: Principles and procedures* (2nd ed.). Boston: Allyn and Bacon.

Winner, M. G., & Crooke, P. (2010). *You are a social detective! Explaining Social Thinking to kids*. San Jose, CA: Think Social Publishing, Inc.

Table of Contents

COPING SKILL TOOLS

Take A Break 7
Take A Break Visuals 9

Strategies 11

Take A Break Schedules 14
Take A Break Schedule Example 15
Take A Break Schedule Template 16

MATERIALS

Target Behaviors 17

Chips 22

BEHAVIOR CHARTS/SELF-MONITORING PLANS

Checkmarks Chart I 26
Checkmarks Chart I Example 27
Checkmarks Chart I Template 28

Checkmarks Chart II 29
Checkmarks Chart II Example 30
Checkmarks Chart II Template 31

Think Chart 32
Think Chart Example 33
Think Chart Template 34

Chip Chart 35
Chip Chart Example 36
Chip Chart Template 37

5 Stamps Chart 38
Five Stamps Chart Example 39
Five Stamps Chart Template 41

Flexibility Chart 43

Stars Chart 46
Stars Chart Example 47
Stars Chart Template 48

Time/Task Chart I 49

Time/Task Chart II 51

DATA RECORDING SHEETS/HOME-SCHOOL COMMUNICATION NOTES

Home-School Communication Notes 53
Daily Boy's Note 54

Daily Boy's Note with Weekly Space Requirement 55
Daily Girl's Note 56
Daily Girl's Note with Weekly Space Requirement 57
Weekly Boy's Note 58
Weekly Girl's Note 59
Weekly Note Without Visual 60
Weekly Note in a Grid 61
Weekly Note for Think Chart 62
Weekly Note for Flexibility Chart 63

REWARDS

Rewards **64**
Reward Ideas 65
Reward Slips 66

Take A Break

Who? Elementary Students, best suited for younger grades

What? Take a Break visuals, space designated in the classroom (within earshot of classroom activities), any items utilized while implementing strategies (i.e., crayons and paper while using drawing as a strategy)

When? Used when needed

Where? School or Home

How? Teaching children how to "Take a Break" (not to be confused with the punishment "Time-out") when they are upset can be an effective way of helping them learn how to regulate their own emotions and behavior. Upon adult suggestion or voluntarily, the child moves away from the group to a place where they still can watch/hear the activity. It gives them an appropriate way to regain self-control and can diffuse a potential outburst. A "Break Card" can be used as a visual to help signal to the child (or for the child to signal to the adult) that he needs a break.

<u>*What might a "Take a Break" space look like?*</u>

- Quiet and comfortable (place a bean bag chair, rocking chair, or soft place to sit in this area)
- Favorite stuffed animal, blanket, soothing item, or 1-2 books
- Bin of calming strategies (labeled using the "Take a Break Bin" visual) including such items as piece of felt cloth, silly putty, squeeze balls, etc. created with child input
- Free of distractions/high energy items (i.e., toys, games, scooters, blank walls, etc.)
- It is helpful for this area to be contained on three sides through the use of walls, partitions, etc.
- Post the "Take a Break Space" sign (see "Take a Break Visuals" page that follows).

How does it work?

- <u>When an adult suggests taking a break to a child, the adult calmly and gently says</u>: "It looks like you are having a tough time (or like you are feeling _____ (frustrated, angry, upset, mad, etc). Take a break." Pair this statement with a break card. (See "Do you want to take a break?" and "Use Break Area" cards that follow on the Take a Break visuals page). This break card serves as a nonverbal signal that prevents or minimizes classroom disruptions. In fact, it can be used as the only communication tool assuming proper discussion has previously taken place regarding the Take a Break space.

- <u>When a child uses the break card, the adult should say:</u> "Great job using your Take a Break card to let me know that you needed a break" or provide similar praise. The child can use the "I'm taking a break" or "BREAK" card (see "Take a Break Visuals" page that follows) by placing it on his desk or by handing it to the adult.

- <u>Note:</u> Children sometimes overuse the time away area when it is first introduced. However, they will begin to use it less when the novelty wears off. Be patient!

Take A Break Visuals

Take a Break Space

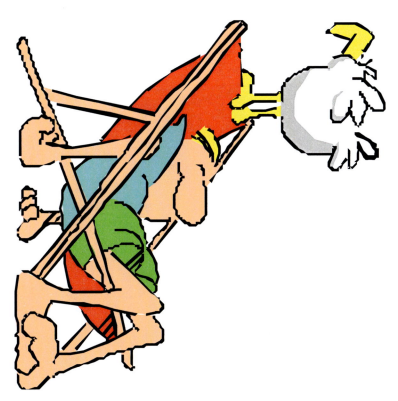

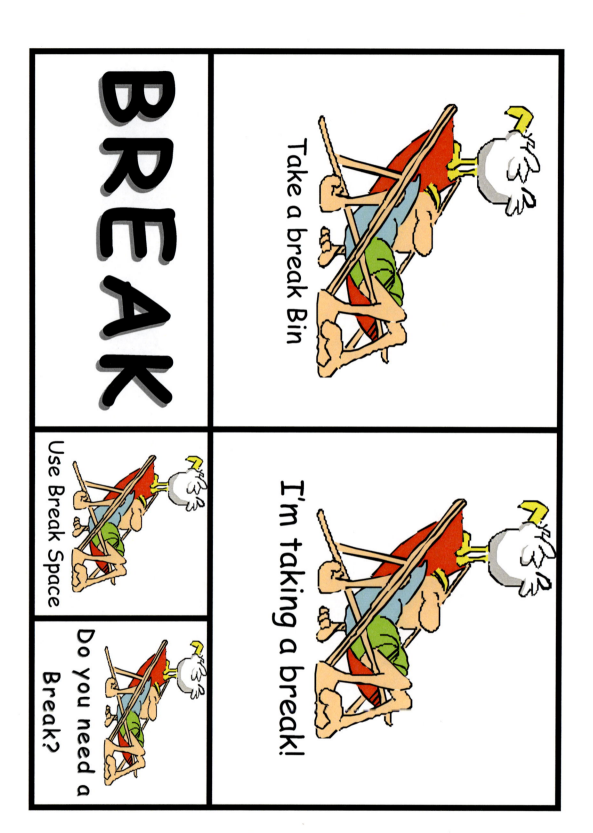

Strategies

These strategies can be used with the "Take a Break" schedules that follow. The strategies can be used to assist students in calming down, in managing their feelings, or in refocusing themselves when distracted. All strategies should be practiced prior to using them. When students are involved in choosing which strategies to include on their "Take a Break" schedules, they are more likely to be invested in using them.

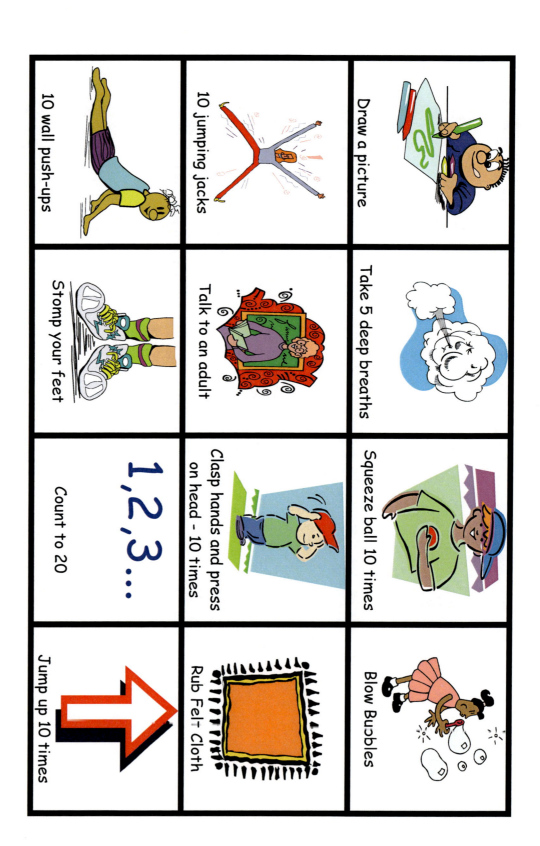

3 minutes	Use Stuffed Animals
5 minutes	Run up/down stairwell
Read a book	Get a drink of water
Listen to music	Talk to a friend

Take A Break Schedules

Who?   Pre-K, Elementary Students

What?   Laminated template, strategy pieces

When?   Used at scheduled times, which the user designates on the chart

Where?   School and home

How?   "Take a Break Schedules" can be used with children who have shown previously that they need frequent breaks and/or are frequently dysregulated. The "Take a Break Schedule" is a preventive strategy that helps a child regain emotional and behavioral control before behavior escalates. The schedule can be set up such that the student takes a break at equal intervals throughout his day or such that specific periods of the day known to be triggers are targeted. At the start of each day, the periods of the day when the breaks will occur are designated in the "When" column. (This can be handwritten on a laminated schedule so that the schedule can be re-used each day or can be used in the future.) When the student is ready to take a designated break, he chooses the length of time by placing either the "3 minutes" or "5 minutes" card under the "How Long?" column in the corresponding block. Finally, the student chooses what kind of strategy he'd like to use. Depending on the child's level of independence, he could be responsible for keeping track of the time or an adult could.

Take A Break Schedule Example

"Take a Break" Schedule

When? (*Note: Breaks take place before or at start of the period below)	How Long?	What kind of break?
Math	3 minutes	Take 5 deep breaths
Science	5 minutes	Run up/down stairwell
Writing	5 minutes	Blow Bubbles

Take A Break Schedule Template

"Take a Break" Schedule

When? (*Note: Breaks take place before or at start of the period below)	How Long?	What kind of break?
	Place Velcro Here	Place Velcro Here
	Place Velcro Here	Place Velcro Here
	Place Velcro Here	Place Velcro Here

Target Behaviors

Target behaviors are the behaviors that are the area of focus or that the child is trying to change. In others words, they are the behaviors that the child hopes to achieve. They are stated in a positive form so that the student knows what the expected behavior is or what the behavior is that they should be showing/exhibiting.

In this book, visuals showing the target behaviors are used on behavior charts/self-monitoring tools in order to serve as a reminder and visual cue of what the child is working on. Target behavior pieces are velcroed to the boxes allotted on each of the behavior charts/self-monitoring tools and left there for the duration of the plan (or until target behaviors change). When using these target behaviors on a chart, it is important to choose no more than 2 or 3 to begin in order to improve the likelihood of success. These target behaviors can be used to customize the Checkmarks Chart I and II, the Think Chart, the Chip Chart, the 5 Stamps Chart, and the Stars Chart.

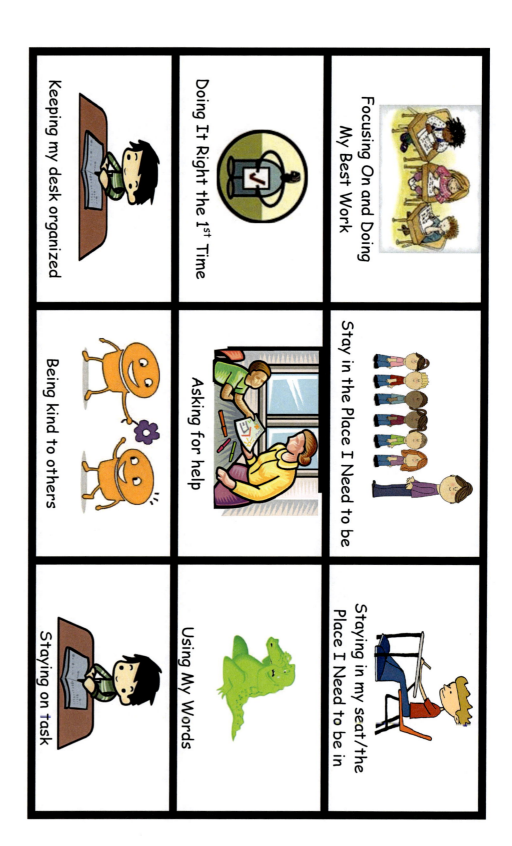

Chips

Chips are used to track data for several of the charts in this book. These chips are used not only to document target behaviors, but also to allow the student to self-monitor these behaviors. The chips are designed to be laminated and cut out in order to be able to velcro them to the chart when in use (and re-use them at a later date). Chips can be stored on the back of the chart using a long strip of Velcro. Storing the chips on the back also allows the chart to become mobile so that it can be used in different settings (i.e., the classroom, learning center, specials, counselor's office, etc.).

The boy/girl chips are used for the Think Chart and the Chip Chart. They also can be used on Checkmarks Chart I and II, and the 5 Stamps Chart as an alternative to checkmarks/stamps. Simply place Velcro pieces in each of the boxes in the 3 "checkmarks" columns or in the 5 blank spaces on the 5 Stamps Chart. Then, instead of writing a checkmark or marking a stamp, add a chip to indicate that the child has exhibited the target behavior. The star chips correspond to the Earning Flexibility Stars Chart.

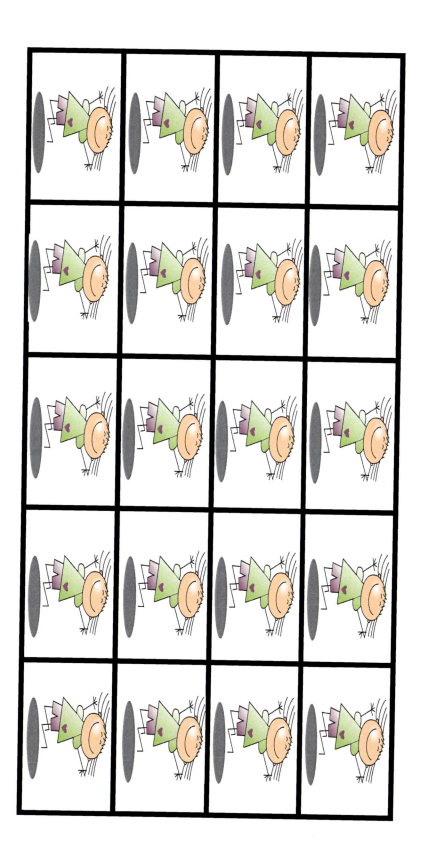

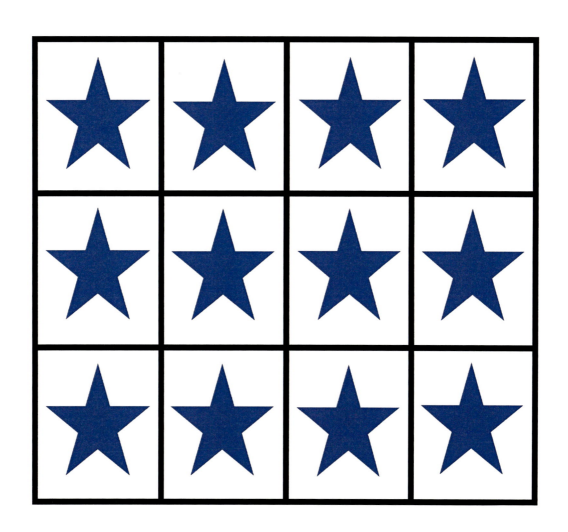

Checkmarks Chart I

Who? Pre-K, Elementary Students, best suited for younger grades

What? Laminated template, target behavior pieces, dry erase markers (to draw checkmarks) (not provided) or chips, stickers (not provided)

When? Used daily

Where? School

How? The Checkmarks Chart consists of 2 sections: one section with an area reserved for attaching target behaviors and the second section with an area reserved for tracking the student's progress on these target behaviors using checkmarks.* During each period of the day (recorded under the "Period" column), the student earns a checkmark for each target behavior displayed throughout that period. It should be noted that the teacher's/counselor's expectations regarding how frequently he displays these behaviors should become more stringent once the student begins to achieve success on the plan. These checkmarks are used not only to document target behaviors, but also to allow the student to self-monitor these behaviors. By providing a sticker for each period that the student earns the full number of possible checkmarks (3) for a given period, the teacher/counselor provides positive reinforcement incrementally. An overall goal is set for a certain number of checkmarks to be earned each day. If the student meets this daily requirement, then he can earn a reward. Once the student demonstrates consistent daily success in meeting his goal (i.e., number of checkmarks earned daily), then his daily requirement goal can be increased.

*NOTE: If using chips instead of writing checkmarks, simply place Velcro pieces in each of the boxes in the 3 "checkmarks" columns

Checkmarks Chart I Example

Name: _____ Date: _____ Checkmarks needed: _____

 Keeping my desk organized	 Listening/Following Directions	 Raising My Hand

Sticker	Period	Checkmarks		
🎈	AM Work	✔	✔	✔
🎈	Reading Group	✔	✔	✔
🎈	Meeting	✔	✔	✔
	Snack		✔	✔
🎈	Writing	✔	✔	✔
🎈	Math	✔	✔	✔
	Meeting	✔		✔
🎈	Specials	✔	✔	✔

Checkmarks Chart I Template

Name: _____ Date: _____ Checkmarks needed: _____

Place Velcro Here	Place Velcro Here	Place Velcro Here

Sticker	Period	Checkmarks		

Checkmarks Chart II

Who?   Elementary Students

What?   Laminated template, target behavior pieces, dry erase markers (to draw checkmarks) (not provided) or chips

When?   Used daily

Where?   School

How?   This chart works the same as Checkmarks Chart I, except it's a bit simpler. There is no "sticker" section. Only checkmarks are used to track target behaviors and to provide reinforcement.* This chart can be used as an alternative to Checkmarks Chart I after a student has become accustomed to using Checkmarks Chart I and no longer requires continuous reinforcement. It also may be preferred for older students who don't require as much reinforcement.

*NOTE: If using chips instead of writing checkmarks, simply place Velcro pieces in each of the boxes in the 3 "checkmarks" columns

Checkmarks Chart II Example

Name: _____ Date: _____ Checkmarks needed: _____

	Keeping my desk organized	Listening/Following Directions	Raising My Hand 
Period	**Checkmarks**		
AM Work	✔	✔	✔
Reading Group	✔	✔	
Meeting	✔	✔	✔
Snack	✔	✔	
Writing	✔	✔	✔
Math	✔	✔	✔
Meeting	✔	✔	✔
Choices		✔	✔

Checkmarks Chart II Template

Name: _____ Date: _____ Checkmarks needed: _____

Place Velcro Here	Place Velcro Here	Place Velcro Here

Period	Checkmarks		

Think Chart

Who? Pre-K, Elementary Students, best suited for younger grades

What? Laminated template, target behavior pieces, chips

When? Used daily

Where? School and home

How? Like Checkmarks Chart I and II, this chart consists of 2 sections: one section with an area reserved for attaching target behaviors and the second section with an area reserved for removing up to 20 chips (either the boy or girl chips from the chips section can be used) throughout the day. When the plan is first implemented, start each day with all 20 chips velcroed on the template. These chips will cover the "think" spaces. Each time he does not exhibit one of the identified target behaviors, a chip is removed from the chart revealing the "think" space, which is an additional nonverbal cue to correct behavior. If the student has at least 1 chip still left on the chart at the end of the day, he has met the daily requirement for earning a reward. Once the student has achieved consistent success on the plan, make the eligibility requirements for a reward more stringent by decreasing the number of chips he starts out with at the beginning of the day. The number of chips that the student starts the day with can be decreased again, once the student has demonstrated consistent success with the new eligibility requirements (i.e., after 2 weeks of consistent performance).

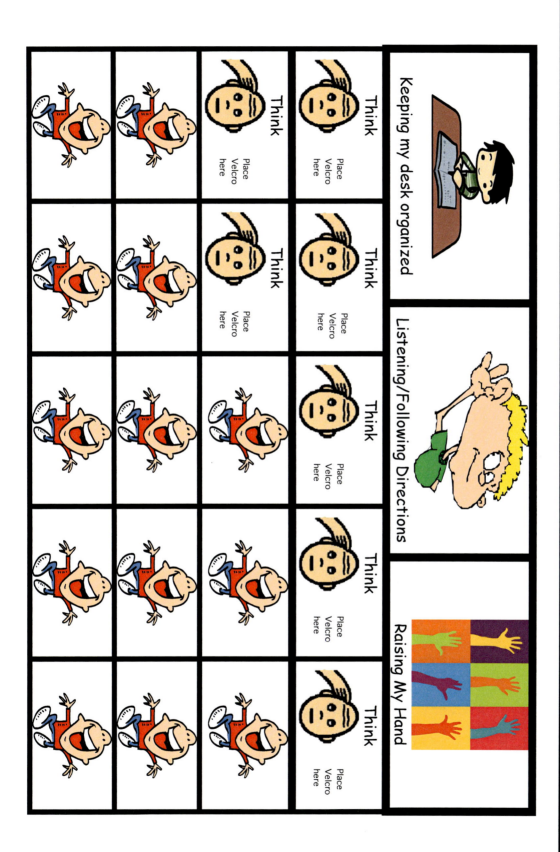

Think Chart Example

Think Chart Template

Think Place Velcro here	Think Place Velcro here	Think Place Velcro here	Think Place Velcro here	Place Velcro Here
Think Place Velcro here	Think Place Velcro here	Think Place Velcro here	Think Place Velcro here	
Think Place Velcro here	Think Place Velcro here	Think Place Velcro here	Think Place Velcro here	Place Velcro Here
Think Place Velcro here	Think Place Velcro here	Think Place Velcro here	Think Place Velcro here	
Think Place Velcro here	Think Place Velcro here	Think Place Velcro here	Think Place Velcro here	Place Velcro Here

Chip Chart

Who?   Pre-K, Elementary Students, best suited for younger grades

What?   Laminated template, target behavior pieces, chips

When?   Used daily

Where?   School and home

How?   After identifying target behaviors and placing these corresponding pieces in the designated boxes, chips can be added throughout the day. Each time the child exhibits one of the identified target behaviors, a chip is added to the chart. Once he has earned 5 chips, he will have met the requirements for a reward. Then, all chips are removed and he begins earning them again. In other words, it is possible for him to earn more than 5 chips/multiple rewards in a day.

Chip Chart Example

If I...

Keeping my desk organized

Listening/Following Directions

Raising My Hand

...I will earn a chip!

Chip Chart Template

If I...

Place Velcro Here

Place Velcro Here

Place Velcro Here

...I will earn a chip!

Place Velcro Here

Place Velcro Here

Place Velcro Here

Place Velcro Here

Place Velcro Here

5 Stamps Chart

Who?   Pre-K, Elementary Students, best suited for younger grades

What?   Laminated template, target behavior pieces, dry erase marker (not provided) to draw the stamps or chips*

When?   Used daily

Where?   School and home

How?   Each time the student exhibits one of the identified target behaviors, a stamp is added to the chart providing positive reinforcement. Once 5 stamps are earned, the student has met the requirements for a reward. Then, a new chart is started and he begins earning them again. In other words, it is possible for him to earn more than 5 stamps in a day. Similarly, stamps can be carried over to the next day. Once the student has earned 5 stamps, a note is made on the documentation sheet indicating that he met the requirement for a reward and which reward he received. Noting the receipt of a reward ensures accountability for providing it. Similarly, noting what the reward is ensures that reward (un)desirability does not impact the plan's effectiveness (e.g., the student is tired of working for the same reward). Given that a student can meet this reward requirement at any point during the day (once the 5 stamps have been earned), an adult should explain when he will receive his reward so that he can anticipate its delivery. Also, it should be noted that adults should use their best judgment to deliver the reward in a timely manner (i.e., by the end of the day, first thing the next morning, etc.) when it can not be provided immediately.

*NOTE: If using chips instead of writing stamps, simply laminate the template and place Velcro pieces in each of the blank spaces where there is a ★ on the example chart.

Five Stamps Chart Example

Date: 11/13/14

My Goals:

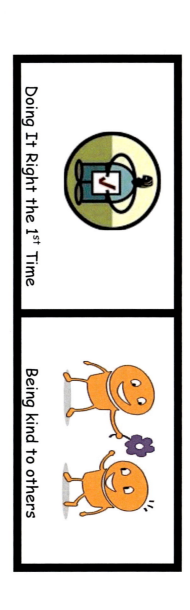

I am working toward: free choice time!

★ ___ + ★ ___ + ★ ___ + ★ ___ + ★ ___ = REWARD!

Please record below each date on which a reward was received (this occurs after 5 stamps/checkmarks have been received):

11/3/14 free choice	11/13/14 free choice							
11/4/14 free choice	11/13/14 free choice							
11/4/14 proud point	11/13/14 free choice							
11/5/14 free choice								
11/6/14 line leader								
11/7/14 free choice								
11/7/14 free choice								
11/10/14 free choice								
11/11/14 lego time								
11/11/14 free choice								
11/11/14 extra job								
11/12/14 free choice								
11/12/14 computer								

Five Stamps Chart Template

Date: _____

My Goals:

Place Velcro Here

Place Velcro Here

I am working toward: _____ !

___ + ___ + ___ + ___ + ___ = **REWARD!**

Please record below each date on which a reward was received (this occurs after 5 stamps/checkmarks have been received):

Flexibility Chart

Who?   Pre-K, Elementary Students, best suited for younger grades

What?   Laminated template, star chips

When?   Used each opportunity that flexible behavior is exhibited

Where?   School and home

How?   This chart is helpful for students who can demonstrate target behaviors for long periods of time, but have specific moments of inflexible behavior. The goal of the Flexibility Chart is to teach a student how to demonstrate more flexible thinking using characters developed by Michelle Garcia Winner and Stephanie Madrigal, in their curriculum *Superflex®... A Superhero Social Thinking® Curriculum* (2008). The two characters, part of a larger Team of Unthinkables, are called "Rock Brain" and "Glassman." Rock Brain causes students to get stuck on their ideas, whereas Glassman causes students to have big reactions to small problems. Both of these characters prevent you from thinking flexibly.

Each time the student demonstrates flexible thinking, he earns a "flexibility star." On the chart, there are 6 strategies listed that he can use to show flexible thinking. When the student is stuck on an idea or is about to have a big reaction, adults can suggest that he use a strategy listed. The adult can say, "This seems like a chance to show flexible thinking. What's your strategy?" If this verbal engagement causes behavior, anxiety, etc. to escalate, an adult can say, "I will give you think time to decide which strategy to use." Then, walk away and return in 1 minute. Upon returning, the adult calmly and gently says, "Which strategy did you choose?" If the child chooses a strategy, a flexibility star will be moved from the back of the chart (where they are stored) to the front of the chart in order to cover whichever Superflex character he defeated. (If the behavior continues to escalate, suggest Taking a Break.*) When all three characters are covered, the student then earns a reward. Depending upon how frequently the student is earning all 3 stars, the student can earn a "tally" or "point" toward a reward in order to provide more frequent reinforcement throughout the day. It should be noted that adults can provide intermittent reinforcement as well by giving a flexibility star when they notice independent flexible thinking. In this case, the example of flexible thinking should be described to the student.

The pictures of Unthinkables from the Superflex curriculum and the list of flexible thinking strategies serve as a reminder and visual cue for both the student and supporting adults. Therefore, when students are taught in therapeutic settings the basic Social Thinking Vocabulary in the first book of the Superflex series, *You Are a Social Detective* (2008) and then are introduced to the Superflex curriculum itself , these Social Thinking tools can be used as an adjunct by educators or service providers to promote flexible thinking across additional settings. With these tools, these adults use the same language across settings and students are reinforced for showing learned flexible thinking skills across settings as well, thereby increasing the likelihood of learned skills being generalized to multiple settings.

*NOTE: See Take a Break section.

Earning Flexibility Stars

Glassman® – I make people have huge reactions.

Rock Brain® – I make people get stuck on their ideas.   **_Rock Brain®_** – I make people get stuck on their ideas.

BEING FLEXIBLE INVOLVES:
1. Doing something even though I might not want to.
2. Accepting a choice that an adult has offered.
3. Moving on, even though I'm frustrated.
4. Accepting help.
5. Stopping even if you are in the best spot.
6. Following directions.

Rock Brain and Glassman © Social Thinking Publishing (2008). All Rights Reserved. Reprinted with permission from Superflex®...A Superhero Social Thinking Curriculum, by Michelle Garcia Winner. www.socialthinking.com

Stars Chart

Who?   Pre-K, Elementary Students, best suited for younger grades

What?   Laminated template, target behavior pieces, dry erase marker (not provided) to draw the stars

When?   Used weekly

Where?   School and home

How?   Using the Stars Chart, the child can earn up to 3 stars each day for exhibiting identified target behaviors. Like previous charts, there is an area designated for placing target behaviors. Below this area is another space for recording stars. Stars can be earned in 2 different ways:

1) For *each target behavior shown* throughout the day, the student earns a star, or

2) For *each segment of the day (beginning, middle, and end of the day)*, the student can earn a star for showing all three of the target behaviors.

To begin, the goal could be to **earn at least 1 star each day**. If this goal is met, the student earns a reward at the end of the week. Once the student maintains success on the plan, the goal can be increased to earning at least 2 stars each day, or earning a specific number of stars throughout the course of the week. A daily or weekly goal can be set in order to earn a reward. Ensure consistent success for a period of time (i.e., 2 weeks) before increasing the requirements for a reward.

Stars Chart Example

This week (11/20/2014) I am working on: _____

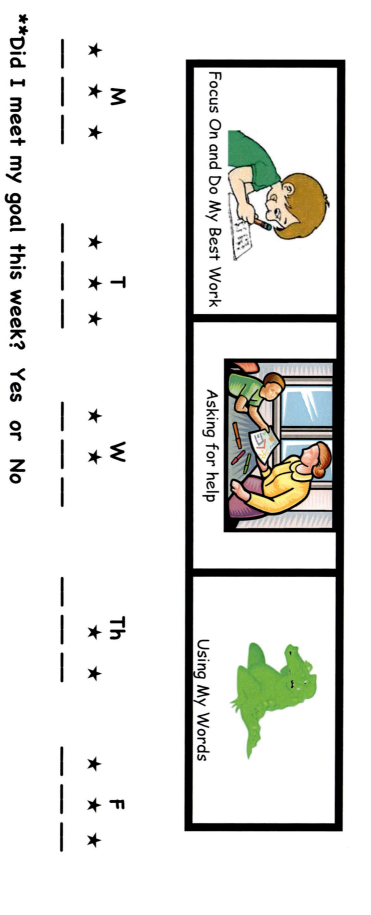

M T W Th F
★★ ★★ ★★ ★★ ★★
★ ★★ ★ ★ ★★★
___ ___ ___ ___ ___

**Did I meet my goal this week? Yes or No

Stars Chart Template

This week (__/__/__) I am working on: _____

M	T	W	Th	F
Place Velcro Here		Place Velcro Here		Place Velcro Here

**Did I meet my goal this week? Yes or No

Time/Task Chart I

Who? Elementary Students, best suited for older grades; particularly helpful for students with attentional and/or executive functioning concerns

What? Laminated template or each week a new sheet can be used (save sheets at the end of the week for data collection and photocopy the page for a home-school communiction note)

When? Used weekly

Where? School

How? Time/Task Charts are used in order to track a specific academic task goal and how much time it is expected to take in order to complete that task. More specifically, the hope is that the student completes that task within the expected amount of time. If he does, then a "yes" is recorded. If he doesn't, a "no" is recorded. The goal can either be for the student to earn a predetermined number of "yes's" each day or during the course of the entire week. Once this goal is met, he earns a reward. It is recommended that any extra "yes's" earned carry over to the next day/week. Although there are enough boxes for 8 possible tasks in a given day, the number of tasks can vary and does not need to be predetermined. These sheets are best suited for independent seat work. It should be noted that an adult can "override" whether or not the time goal is met. In other words, if the student did not complete the entire task goal, but showed a concerted effort to do so, the adult can record a "yes" and make a note about the exception. This caveat is important to make because sometimes a student works conscientiously and diligently, but for whatever reason (i.e., task goal is too ambitious, student focused on high quality, etc.) does not meet the task goal, despite showing a concerted effort.

WEEK OF: _____   GOAL MET?: _____   Yes's = Reward.
Highlight boxes in yellow when applying them toward reward.

	Task #1	Task #2	Task #3	Task #4	Task #5	Task #6	Task #7	Task #8
Monday	Goal: Goal Time: Goal Met? Y or N	Goal: Goal Time: Goal Met? Y or N	Goal: Goal Time: Goal Met? Y or N	Goal: Goal Time: Goal Met? Y or N	Goal: Goal Time: Goal Met? Y or N	Goal: Goal Time: Goal Met? Y or N	Goal: Goal Time: Goal Met? Y or N	Goal: Goal Time: Goal Met? Y or N
Tuesday	Goal: Goal Time: Goal Met? Y or N	Goal: Goal Time: Goal Met? Y or N	Goal: Goal Time: Goal Met? Y or N	Goal: Goal Time: Goal Met? Y or N	Goal: Goal Time: Goal Met? Y or N	Goal: Goal Time: Goal Met? Y or N	Goal: Goal Time: Goal Met? Y or N	Goal: Goal Time: Goal Met? Y or N
Wednesday	Goal: Goal Time: Goal Met? Y or N	Goal: Goal Time: Goal Met? Y or N	Goal: Goal Time: Goal Met? Y or N	Goal: Goal Time: Goal Met? Y or N	Goal: Goal Time: Goal Met? Y or N	Goal: Goal Time: Goal Met? Y or N	Goal: Goal Time: Goal Met? Y or N	Goal: Goal Time: Goal Met? Y or N
Thursday	Goal: Goal Time: Goal Met? Y or N	Goal: Goal Time: Goal Met? Y or N	Goal: Goal Time: Goal Met? Y or N	Goal: Goal Time: Goal Met? Y or N	Goal: Goal Time: Goal Met? Y or N	Goal: Goal Time: Goal Met? Y or N	Goal: Goal Time: Goal Met? Y or N	Goal: Goal Time: Goal Met? Y or N
Friday	Goal: Goal Time: Goal Met? Y or N	Goal: Goal Time: Goal Met? Y or N	Goal: Goal Time: Goal Met? Y or N	Goal: Goal Time: Goal Met? Y or N	Goal: Goal Time: Goal Met? Y or N	Goal: Goal Time: Goal Met? Y or N	Goal: Goal Time: Goal Met? Y or N	Goal: Goal Time: Goal Met? Y or N

Time/Task Chart II

Who? Elementary Students, best suited for older grades

What? Laminated template or each week a new sheet can be used (save sheets each day for data
collection and photocopy the page for a home-school communiction note)

When? Used daily

Where? School

How? Like Time/Task Chart I, this one also is used in order to track a specific academic task goal and how much time it is expected to take in order to complete that task. More specifically, the hope is that the student completes that task within the expected amount of time. If he does, then a "yes" is recorded. If he doesn't, a "no" is recorded. Once a student earns a predetermined number of yes's, he earns a reward. It is recommended that once a student reaches this predetermined number of yes's and earns the reward, any additional yes's from the day be carried over to the next day. Although there are enough boxes for 5 possible tasks in a given day, the number of tasks can vary and does not need to be predetermined. Like Time/Task Chart I, these sheets also are best suited for independent seat work. The same caveat that is applied to Time/Task Chart I, can be applied here. An adult can "override" whether or not the time goal is met. In other words, if the student did not complete the entire task goal, but showed a concerted effort to do so, the adult can record a "yes" and make a note about the exception. This caveat is important to make because sometimes a student works conscientiously and diligently, but for whatever reason (i.e., task goal is too ambitious, student focused on high quality, etc.) does not meet the task goal, despite showing a concerted effort.

Date: _____

	Task #1	Task #2	Task #3	Task #4	Task #5
Goal					
Goal Time					
Was Goal Completed within Goal Time?	Yes or No	Yes or No	Yes or No	Yes or No	Yes or No

Reward Requirement met (please circle one)? *Yes* **or** *Not Yet*

What is the reward? _____

When was it received? _____

Home-School Communication Notes

- Home-school notes are a helpful way of keeping caregivers informed of student progress.
- Notes can be sent home on a daily or a weekly basis. Establishing a consistent, predictable schedule is important.
- Home-school notes can be photocopied or data can be transcribed onto a duplicate sheet to serve as documentation. In other words, the home-school notes can be used simultaneously as a data-recording sheet as well.
- Notes with "comments" sections allow for both quantitative and qualitative data to be provided.
- Since Time-task Chart I & II are data-recording sheets in and of themselves, they can simply be photocopied and sent home.
- The 5 Stamps chart has a data collection sheet that can simply be photocopied and sent home as well.
- The following is a table of charts with compatible home-school notes:

	Checkmarks Chart 1	Checkmarks Chart 2	Think Chart	Chip Chart	Stars Chart	Flexibility Chart
Daily boys' note	✓	✓		✓	✓	
Daily boys' note with weekly requirement space	✓	✓		✓	✓	
Daily girls' note	✓	✓		✓	✓	
Daily girls' note with weekly requirement space	✓	✓		✓	✓	
Weekly boys' note	✓	✓			✓	
Weekly girls' note	✓	✓			✓	
Weekly note without visual	✓	✓			✓	
Weekly note in a grid	✓	✓			✓	
Weekly note for Think chart			✓			
Weekly note for flexibility plan						✓

Daily Boy's Note

Date: _____

Did I meet my goal?

Yes or No

Reward earned: _____

Comments: _____
_____
_____
_____

(Daily Home/School Note for: _____)

Daily Boy's Note with Weekly Space Requirement

Weekday: _____

| Did I meet today's Goal? Y or N |

Comments: _____
_____

Weekly requirement met (if final day of the week)? Y or N
(Daily Home/School Note for: _____)

Daily Girl's Note

Date: _____

Did I meet my goal?

Yes   or   No

Reward earned: _____

Comments: _____
_____
_____
_____

(Daily Home/School Note for: _____)

Daily Girl's Note with Weekly Space Requirement

Weekday: _____

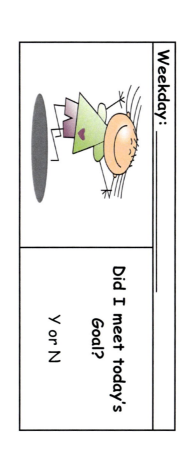

Did I meet today's Goal?

Y or N

Comments: _____
_____

Weekly requirement met (if final day of the week)?   Y   or   N

(Daily Home/School Note for: _____)

Weekly Boy's Note

Week of: _____	Monday	Tuesday	Wednesday	Thursday	Friday
	Y or N	Y or N	Y or N	Y or N	Y or N

Comments: _____
_____
_____
_____

Weekly Reward Earned?   Y or N   (Weekly Home/School Note for: _____)

Weekly Girl's Note

Week of: _____	Monday	Tuesday	Wednesday	Thursday	Friday
	Y or N	Y or N	Y or N	Y or N	Y or N

Comments: _____
_____
_____
_____

Weekly Reward Earned?   Y or N   (Weekly Home/School Note for: _____)

Weekly Note Without Visual

Week of:	Monday	Tuesday	Wednesday	Thursday	Friday
Met goals?	Y or N	Y or N	Y or N	Y or N	Y or N

Weekly requirement met (Fridays only)? Y or N

Comments: _____
_____
_____
_____
_____
_____

(Daily Home/School Note for: _____)

Weekly Note in a Grid

Student's Name: _____   Week of: _____

	Did I meet my goal?		Comments
Monday	Yes	No	
Tuesday	Yes	No	
Wednesday	Yes	No	
Thursday	Yes	No	
Friday	Yes	No	

Reward earned? _____   Date Reward was Received: _____

Weekly Note for Think Chart

Please circle the appropriate amount or rating where appropriate:

Week of: _____

	M	T	W	Th	F
# of chips remaining	0 1 2 3 4 5 6 7 8 9 10 11 12 13 14 15 16 17 18 19 20	0 1 2 3 4 5 6 7 8 9 10 11 12 13 14 15 16 17 18 19 20	0 1 2 3 4 5 6 7 8 9 10 11 12 13 14 15 16 17 18 19 20	0 1 2 3 4 5 6 7 8 9 10 11 12 13 14 15 16 17 18 19 20	0 1 2 3 4 5 6 7 8 9 10 11 12 13 14 15 16 17 18 19 20
Goal Met?	Yes or No	Yes or No	Yes or No	Yes or No	Yes or No

Weekly Note for Flexibility Chart

Data Sheet

Week of: ___	M	T	W	Th	F
# of stars earned	0 1 2 3 4 5 6 7 8 9 10	0 1 2 3 4 5 6 7 8 9 10	0 1 2 3 4 5 6 7 8 9 10	0 1 2 3 4 5 6 7 8 9 10	0 1 2 3 4 5 6 7 8 9 10
Top Flexible Thinking Skill Shown	___ Tried another way to solve a problem (defeated Rock Brain) ___ Showed a reaction that met size of the problem (defeated Glassman)	___ Tried another way to solve a problem (defeated Rock Brain) ___ Showed a reaction that met size of the problem (defeated Glassman)	___ Tried another way to solve a problem (defeated Rock Brain) ___ Showed a reaction that met size of the problem (defeated Glassman)	___ Tried another way to solve a problem (defeated Rock Brain) ___ Showed a reaction that met size of the problem (defeated Glassman)	___ Tried another way to solve a problem (defeated Rock Brain) ___ Showed a reaction that met size of the problem (defeated Glassman)

Comments: _____

(Home/School Note for: _____)

Rewards

- All rewards should be provided at the teacher's discretion in order to ensure that they do not interfere with the classroom routine.
- Certain items (i.e., free homework pass) can be reserved for exceptional behavior and/or given at the teacher's discretion as well.
- If tangible items (i.e., prize box) are used, switching to a social reinforcer or other non-tangible reward (i.e., proud points, extra recess, computer time with a friend, etc.) is suggested after "buy-in" has been firmly established.
- It is important to establish a predictable, consistent time (i.e., at the end of each day) that the reward will be provided so that the student knows when to expect it.

Reward Ideas

1. Computer time (10 min.) (may not be possible every time it is requested and must be coordinated with the teacher)
2. Helping the office staff
3. 10 extra min. of reading time.
4. 10 min. to work on an arts and crafts project.
5. Free time (10 min.)
6. Free time with a friend (10 min)
7. Being 1st in line.
8. Having an extra job.
9. Getting to choose your job.
10. Teacher's choice.
11. Extra (indoor) recess time (10 min.) with a friend.
12. Lunch with teacher/adult in the school.
13. Telling a joke in front of the class
14. Prize box.
15. Show and tell or sharing time (bringing in an object from home to present to the class)
16. Being the teacher (student is allowed to "be the teacher" for a predetermined amount of time)
17. Extra recess time for the entire class
18. Free Homework Pass
19. Class Spirit Day (i.e., Pajama Day, Opposite Day, Crazy Hat Day, etc.)
20. Sitting in the teacher's chair for one period, day, etc.

Reward Slips

Computer time with a friend!

Chosen on: _____

Received on: _____

Arts & Crafts time!

Chosen on: _____

Received on: _____

Game time with a friend!

Chosen on: _____

Received on: _____

Choosing your job!
Chosen on: _____   Received on: _____

Extra recess time!
Chosen on: _____   Received on: _____

Borrowing a game from the classroom/office!
Chosen on: _____   Received on: _____

Telling a joke in front of the class!
Chosen on: _____   Received on: _____

Show and tell to the class/sharing time!
Chosen on: _____
Received on: _____

Sitting in teacher's chair!
Chosen on: _____
Received on: _____

10 proud points for the class!
Chosen on: _____
Received on: _____

Extra Job! ☺
Chosen on: _____
Received on: _____

Choice of 1st or last in line! ☺

Chosen on: _____

Received on: _____

Lunch with a teacher! ☺

Chosen on: _____

Received on: _____

Computer Time! ☺

Chosen on: _____

Received on: _____

Free Time! ☺

Chosen on: _____

Received on: _____

Lego Time! ☺

Chosen on: _____ Received on: _____

Time to write/draw in your special notebook! ☺

Chosen on: _____ Received on: _____

Chosen on: _____ Received on: _____ ☺

Made in the USA
Middletown, DE
08 June 2016